S0-BNE-802

J
508
Tho
Thomson
Winter

5614540
10.80

DATE DUE			

mo

GREAT RIVER REGIONAL LIBRARY

St. Cloud, Minnesota   56301

GAYLORD M2G

Get set... GO!

Winter

Ruth Thomson

Contents

CHILDRENS PRESS®

CHICAGO

S614540

It's winter!

Winter days are short and cold.
It is often snowy and icy.
The trees are bare and the
ground is often frozen.

It is hard for animals and birds
to find food.
There are no green shoots or leaves.
There are no flying insects.

Some birds fly to warmer places
in the autumn.
Birds that stay behind feed on
seeds and berries.

Bats and chipmunks sleep through
the winter in a sheltered place.
Foxes and deer are active all winter.
They grow thicker coats to keep warm.

3

Look at winter buds

Get ready

✔ Notebook   ✔ Pencil

Horse Chestnut

. . . Get Set

Look at some tree buds
in your yard or in a park.
Notice their size, shape, and color.
See how the buds are arranged—
singly, in pairs, or in clusters.

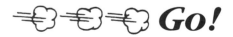 *Go!*

Draw some of the twigs you find.
Make notes about the buds.
Even when trees are bare, you will
soon recognize them by their buds.

The buds are in opposite pairs.

Scar from last year's leaf stalk.

Willow: The grey, furry buds are arranged singly.

Ash: The black, pointed buds are arranged in pairs.

Birch: These are catkins (birch flowers). The pointed buds are arranged alternately.

Plane: The rounded buds are arranged alternately.

Lime: The twigs are a zigzag shape. There is a bud at each joint.

A twig squirrel

Get ready

✔ Bendy twigs   ✔ Dried flowers

✔ Ivy stripped of leaves   ✔ Nuts

. . . Get Set

Make two balls of bendy twigs
for the head and body.
Push short twigs into the body
with the ends showing.
Fix the head onto them.

≈💨≈💨≈💨 *Go!*

Bind some short twigs with ivy.
Push them into the head and body
to make the ears and legs.
Bind in dried flowers for the tail.
Push in nuts for the eyes and nose.

Twig weaving

Get ready

✔ 3 big twigs
✔ String
✔ Smaller twigs and stalks

✔ Green twine
✔ Pinecones
✔ Rosehips and other berries

✔ Feathers
✔ Leaves

. . . Get Set

Tie the three big twigs together with string to make a triangle.

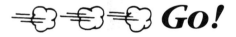 **Go!**

Tie the smaller twigs and stalks across the triangle with twine. Weave other twigs in lengthwise. Put pinecones, feathers, berries, leaves, and other things you find into the gaps. Use your weaving as a holiday decoration.

Advent candles

Get ready

- ✔ Stiff cardboard
- ✔ Aluminum foil
- ✔ Glue
- ✔ 4 candleholders

- ✔ Silver balls
- ✔ Sprigs of fir and holly
- ✔ Big pinecone

- ✔ Gold paint
- ✔ Paintbrush
- ✔ 4 candles

. . . Get Set

Cut a large circle of cardboard.
Cover it with aluminum foil.

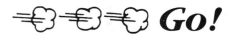 **Go!**

Glue the candleholders onto the foil.
Surround them with silver balls,
holly, and sprigs of fir.
Paint the pinecone gold and put it
in the center of your display.
Put the candles in the holders.

Snowflakes

Get ready

- ✔ Thin white paper
- ✔ Teacup
- ✔ Pencil
- ✔ Safety scissors
- ✔ Transparent tape

. . . Get Set

Put the cup on the paper. Draw around it. Cut out the circle. Fold it in half, making a semi-circle. Fold the semi-circle in thirds to make a cone shape.

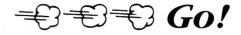 **Go!**

Snip shapes in all the edges. Unfold the paper. Tape your snowflake to a window.

Cake for the birds

Get ready

- ✔ Scraps of cooked rice, pasta, or potato
- ✔ Lard (½ cup)
- ✔ Ovenproof pan
- ✔ Seeds and nuts
- ✔ Raisins
- ✔ Plastic cup
- ✔ String

. . . Get Set

Put the lard in the pan.
Ask an adult to
melt it in the oven.
Stir in the food scraps.

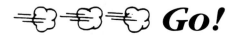 *Go!*

Pierce a hole in the cup.
Thread the string through.
Knot the end to fix it inside the cup.
Spoon the food mixture into the cup.
Put it in the refrigerator to harden.
Unmold the cake and hang it up outdoors.

Stick monster

Get ready

- ✔ Stick with an odd shape
- ✔ Sandpaper
- ✔ Paints
- ✔ Paintbrush

. . . Get Set

Look for an oddly shaped stick
that could be made into a monster.

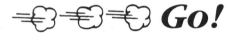 ## Go!

Brush off any loose bits of bark.
Rub the stick with sandpaper
until it is smooth.
Paint it in bright colors.
It may need several coats of paint.

Stone pictures

Get ready

✔ Some small
 stones
✔ Cardboard

✔ Pencil
✔ White glue

. . . Get Set

Collect some small stones
on your next winter walk.

〓🗨〓🗨〓🗨 *Go!*

Draw an outline on the cardboard—
a bird, an animal, or another shape.
Glue the stones all over it
to make a mosaic.

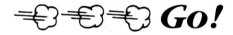

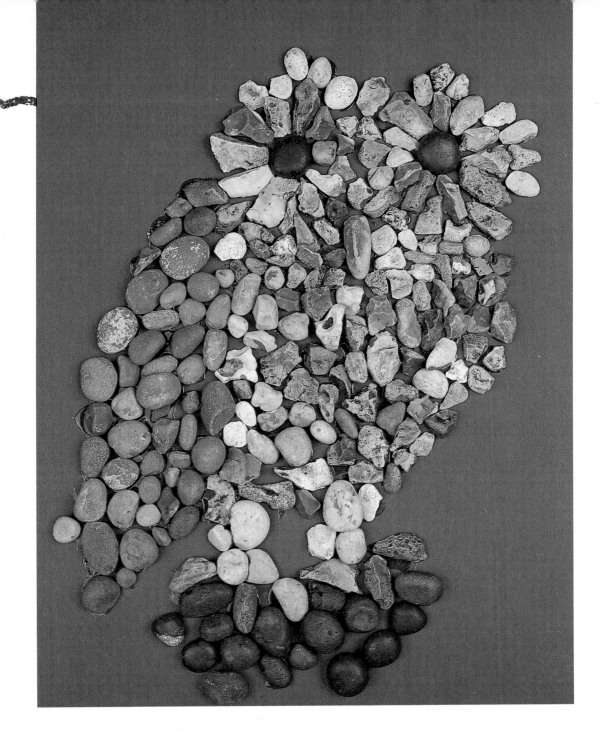

Finger puppets

Get ready

✔ Pencil   ✔ Needle and thread   ✔ Safety scissors

✔ Cardboard   ✔ Felt or fur fabric   ✔ Glue

. . . Get Set

Lay one of your fingers on the
cardboard and draw around it.
Draw another line about 1 inch away.
Cut along the outside line.

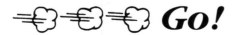 *Go!*

Use the cardboard pattern
to cut two pieces of fabric.
Sew them together,
leaving the bottom edges open.
Sew or glue on eyes, nose, ears,
paws, and tail.

A festive wreath

Get ready

✔ Straw, wire, or basketware ring

✔ Soft wire

✔ Pruning shears

✔ Sprays of evergreen leaves

✔ Shiny balls

✔ Bells

✔ Pinecones

✔ Red ribbon

. . . Get Set

Bind sprays of holly, ivy, and
other evergreens all around
the ring with soft wire.
Ask an adult to cut the wire for you.

 **Go!**

Tie some shiny balls, bells, and
pinecones onto the wreath with wire.
Make a huge ribbon bow and
fix it at the bottom with more wire.

Index

Photographic credits: Heather Angel, 3;
Chris Fairclough Colour Library 19, 21;
Peter Millard, 4, 5, 7, 9, 11, 13, 15, 17, 23

Editor: Pippa Pollard
Design: Ruth Levy
Cover design: Mike Davis
Artwork: Ruth Levy

Library of Congress Cataloging-in-Publication Data
Thomson, Ruth.
    Winter / by Ruth Thomson.
      p.   cm. — (Get set— go!)
    Includes index.
    ISBN 0-516-07997-2
    1. Nature craft—Juvenile literature. 2. Handicraft—Juvenile
literature. [1. Winter. 2. Nature craft. 3. Handicraft.] I. Title.
II. Series.
TT157.T52   1994
508—dc20   94-12307
                                      CIP
                                      AC

1994 Childrens Press® Edition
© 1993 Watts Books, London, New York, Sydney
All rights reserved. Printed in the United States of America.
Published simultaneously in Canada.
1 2 3 4 5 6 7 8 9 0 R 03 02 01 00 99 98 97 96 95 94

24